BUSINESS SURVIVAL
IN THE SIXTIES

THE CHARLES C. MOSKOWITZ LECTURES

The Moskowitz Lectures have been established through the generosity of a distinguished alumnus of the School of Commerce, Mr. Charles C. Moskowitz of the Class of 1914, who retired after many years as Vice President-Treasurer and Director of Loew's, Inc.

In establishing the lectures, it was Mr. Moskowitz's aim to contribute to the understanding of the function of business and its underlying disciplines in society by providing a public forum for the dissemination of enlightened business theories and practices.

The School of Commerce, Accounts, and Finance and New York University are deeply grateful to Mr. Moskowitz for his continued interest in, and contribution to, the educational and public service program of his alma mater.

BUSINESS SURVIVAL
IN THE SIXTIES

THOMAS F. PATTON
PRESIDENT
REPUBLIC STEEL CORPORATION

The Charles C. Moskowitz Lectures
School of Commerce, Accounts, and Finance
New York University

HARPER & BROTHERS · *Publishers*
New York

CONTENTS
1162650

FOREWORD

To inaugurate the Moskowitz Lectures, the School of Commerce was indeed fortunate in having Mr. Thomas F. Patton deliver the first series of three lectures, on the general theme, *Business Survival in the Sixties*—a decade which promises to be one of the most critical in America's history.

Mr. Patton is well qualified to speak of the great problems facing business in the years ahead. As president and chief executive officer of Republic Steel Corporation, the nation's third largest steel producer, he will be one of the important and responsible business leaders of the next decade.

In addition, since his graduation from The Ohio State University with a Bachelor of Laws in 1926, Mr. Patton has been interested in higher education. Today he serves as a member of the Board of Trustees of his alma mater and, as such, recognizes the part which higher education must play in our future.

His breadth of interests, however, has not been confined to the law, business, and education. Long active in the civic and charitable affairs of Greater Cleveland, Mr. Patton is past chairman and trustee of the Cleveland Development Foundation, past chairman of the Cleveland Chamber of Commerce, and a trustee and officer of many civic, charitable, and cultural organizations. He holds honorary doctorates from Cleveland-Marshall Law School, John Carroll University, and the University of Dayton.

In these three lectures he brings to bear on the business problems ahead, both at home and abroad, the breadth of background so essential to the modern successful business executive. The range of his discussion of these problems, the ways of meeting these challenges, and the opportunities they afford, should be required reading for all who will share the responsibility for making America an even greater nation.

Thomas L. Norton, Dean
School of Commerce, Accounts, and Finance
New York University

INTRODUCTION

If this series of lectures had been given in the Spring of 1960, the prevailing enthusiasm for the "Golden Sixties" would have made me overly optimistic about the decade that lies ahead. Today, with business at a lower level, it would be just as easy to be unduly pessimistic about the future.

I think we should remember that in business, as in the stock market, conditions are seldom as good or as bad as they seem. We are entering a new era, and we should have faith in that era. But the sobering experience of the last half of 1960 should encourage a more realistic appraisal of the problems and challenges that lie ahead. One thing is certain: if the past year is prologue to the future, business management will face difficult problems and revolutionary changes as well as dynamic challenges and unsurpassed opportunities throughout the coming decade. Therefore, if companies like ours are to survive, compete, and grow, businessmen much reach new levels of managerial competence.

In preparing these lectures I have selected those problems and challenges that will most likely affect our progress as business enterprises in a free society. I have drawn heavily upon our experience in the steel industry, but the examples used have been chosen because of their relevance to other industries as well.

The first lecture will be devoted to our management problems at home, the second will deal with problems abroad, and the third will suggest a strategy for business survival.

ACKNOWLEDGMENT

By providing a forum for the discussion of business problems and policies, Mr. Charles C. Moskowitz and New York University have rendered a great service to the business community and the nation. I am highly honored to have been chosen to deliver the first series of three lectures.

I want to express my appreciation to the many people who contributed information needed in the preparation of these lectures. I am particularly indebted to my Republic Steel associates William P. Carlin, L. C. Michelon, and James E. Payne for their advice and assistance.

Thomas F. Patton

BUSINESS SURVIVAL
IN THE SIXTIES

THE PROBLEMS FOR
MANAGEMENT AT HOME

THE IDEOLOGICAL CHALLENGE

I am sure that all of us want to preserve our free enterprise system and democratic way of life. The underlying values of our free society are the only dependable yardsticks against which we can measure the problems of the future and chart our course of action.

Therefore, all of the problems I discuss and all of the alternatives I propose will be examined in terms of freedom of choice, private property, profit incentives, competition, and democratic government. These ingredients of our economic and political climate are essential to long-term business growth in the American tradition.

Frankly, I am concerned about the ideological road we have been traveling. We do not need mental radar to see that our goals have been blurred and that we have lost some of the direction and purpose of the Founding Fathers.

Can we say that the average American today feels a sense of mission? That he is guided by clearly understood and accepted economic and political values? I am sure that most of us subscribe to the broad principles of democracy and free enterprise, but how many of us look beneath the surface to see if we are living up to these principles?

1

This is a serious problem, and it can be solved only through sound economic and political education. This places an awesome responsibility upon business management as well as upon our high schools and colleges.

The ideological challenge is staggering when you realize how little our people know about free enterprise and democratic government. At Republic we have tested thousands of employees prior to their taking economic and political courses. Our written questionnaires are anonymous and are intended to elicit both knowledge and opinions.

Here are some typical scores before training:

87 per cent had no clear idea of the kind of government the Constitution sets up

60 per cent believed labor is the only productive factor

59 per cent believed all increases in productivity should be paid out in higher wages

45 per cent believed Communism needs no capital

34 per cent believed the electoral college is a special school for congressmen's children!

This is no laughing matter. The lack of knowledge is not limited to industrial employees. In 1958, a university professor submitted ten questions to ninety of his students with these results:

Eight knew precisely what was meant by the Bill of Rights

Four had heard of a "right-to-work" law

Estimates on the national debt ranged from $1 million to $500 billion!

These results are not surprising when you consider that less than one-third of our college students and fewer than one-tenth of our high school students take even one course in economics!

To be vigorous in our defense of free ideas we must have a good grasp of the underlying values of our society. We cannot talk sensibly about problems or challenges or solutions until we know the values we want to preserve. Freedom demands eternal vigilance, but vigilance based on economic and political understanding. That is why Thomas Jefferson said: "If a nation expects to be ignorant and free it expects what never was and never will be."

We at Republic Steel believe that business should help carry economic and political education to all its people—and we are practicing what we preach. In the past ten years we have given courses in economic education to almost ten thousand supervisors and hourly employees. In 1960 alone we provided fifteen conferences and workshops in political science. These were attended voluntarily by more than three thousand men and women on their own time, off the company's premises, and in their own home communities.

We feel we must do what we can to build public understanding and support for the way of life that has led us on to freedom and fortune throughout our history.

This is particularly important today because of the second great problem that is looming on the horizon: the population explosion.

THE POPULATION EXPLOSION

In 1960 our population officially passed the 182 million mark. This represented an increase of 30 million people in ten years. By 1970 our population will jump another 30 million, and it may reach 270 million by 1980. This would be an increase of 90 million people in twenty years—a whopping 50 per cent.

By the end of the decade it is estimated that we will have:

A population of 212 million

An increase in the labor force from 73 to 87 million

A rise in school enrollment from 47 million to 57 million

An increase in the number of families from 45 to 52 million

A sharp rise to 20 million in the number of people 65 or older.

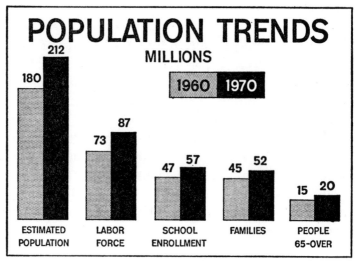

FIG. 1   Population Trends

When some people look ahead to this population explosion, all they see is an expanding market and a booming economy—more houses and cars, longer vacations and shorter work weeks, and more leisure time. But India, China, Africa, and South America are living proof that

4

population growth without a corresponding economic growth is a danger rather than a guarantee of progress. Productive capacity and job opportunities must keep pace if population growth is to lead to expanding markets and higher living standards.

This poses a particular problem for America. By 1965 we will be challenged to provide suitable jobs for the flood of young people who will be joining our labor force. Because of the baby boom after World War II, the number of young workers under 25 will *increase 46 per cent* during the Sixties.

The crest of this wave of young workers will hit the labor force with greatest impact in 1965. In that year alone about 4 million young people will reach the age of 18— an increase of nearly 50 per cent over the year 1960. Many of these young men and women will enter college, some will go into the armed services, but the rest will come to our employment offices looking for jobs.

In another sense, however, this flood of students and young workers represents an exciting opportunity. Here are the thousands of scientists we need to light the way for generations to come. Here are the thousands of new engineers needed to translate the findings of science into productive machines and processes. Here are tomorrow's entrepreneurs—the businessmen who will fill the growing demand for goods and services. Here, too, are the future doctors, lawyers, farmers, and steelworkers. Here, in short, are the men and women who will adapt the treasures of the earth to the service of mankind.

Their minds and their skills are the greatest wealth in our land. To falter before the task of developing this mine of talent would be the rankest folly. One man hired in the Sixties may prove to be a Thomas Edison or a Louis Pasteur. Ten men from the class of 1965 may make discoveries worth the cost of educating their entire generation!

But while we are looking at these potentials we must not forget that increased population will bring on many other problems as well. For example:

About 75 per cent of our people will live in about 170 highly congested metropolitan areas

Increased marriages and rapid family formation will increase the pressure for public housing, public utilities, and social services

Population growth will cause an epidemic of crimes, even if the crime *rate* remains the same

The expansion of our older age group will increase the need for hospitals, mental institutions, and recreational facilities

Finally, the large number of young people will increase the demand for more and better schools.

When you put all of these problems together, the implied load on all levels of government—and on every individual—is going to be far greater than it is today. Federal, state, and local governments will spend approximately $170 billion in 1970—more than *twice the entire national income for 1940.*

On top of that, the population explosion will be complicated by the mobility of our people. Americans are a restless people. Every year, one out of every five of us moves down the hall, across the street, or even across the country. We are making building lots out of farm land. We are developing our last frontiers. As a result, the South, the Southwest, the Far West, and the Northwest are experiencing regional growth of massive proportions. To meet the needs of this vast population on the move, industry must decentralize and increase the flexibility of its production facilities.

A good example is the steel plant in Gadsden, Alabama, which Republic acquired in 1937. At that time the southeastern states serviced by the plant were primarily agricultural states. Their steel demands were small. Since then, however, they have experienced tremendous growth. To supply their needs we have had to rebuild our steel plant,

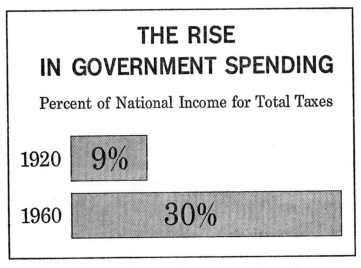

FIG. 2   The Rise in Government Spending

expand its facilities, and change its product mix. We have built new blast furnaces, open hearths, and electric furnaces; we have added a large-diameter pipe mill, a strip mill, a galvanizing plant, and a wider plate mill, and we are now installing a new sintering plant.

This points up one conclusion: in an economy such as ours, population and industry must grow together.

7

The population explosion of the Sixties will also create problems in the public sector of our economy. Government tends to grow with population, too. Unless we are vigilant there could well be a drift toward government dominance at the expense of the individual and private enterprise.

We have already gone far in that direction. In 1920, federal, state, and local governments taxed away and spent only 9 per cent of our national income. Today they take almost 30 per cent and the upward trend is continuing. If we are going to provide for our future public needs without crippling the personal and corporate incentives built into our economy, we must attract highly qualified people into government who will strive for maximum foresight and efficiency.

Here, too, business must do its share. It will no longer be enough for the businessman to concern himself with the technical problems of production and distribution, or to limit his political activity to financial contributions to the party of his choice. He must be a publicist, an educator, and a crusader for the principles upon which this nation was founded. And, like all citizens of a free society, he must ask himself these important questions:

Am I taking an active part in public affairs?

Am I insisting on sound fiscal policies?

Am I speaking up against legislation which would impair the general business climate?

Am I planning to work harder and more effectively in public affairs in the decade ahead?

Everyone must do his share if we are going to satisfy the public needs dictated by our rapidly growing population—and do it without weakening or destroying the basic features of our society.

THE NEED FOR ECONOMIC GROWTH

The third great domestic problem we face is that of providing the long-term economic growth dictated by our expanding population. Last year we became the first country in history to produce a Gross National Product of $500 billion. This was a mighty achievement when you consider the downturn in business during the second half of the year.

A Gross National Product of $750 billion is predicted for 1970. This would represent a rise of 50 per cent in just ten years. This seems almost incredible until you begin to think in terms of people and markets. Babies are coming along at the rate of over four million a year, and most of them grow up, are profitably employed, and become customers. It has been estimated that, among other things, four million babies use up during their lifetimes:

    1 billion pairs of shoes
   25 billion pounds of beef
   63 million suits and dresses
   11 million new cars
   91 billion gallons of gasoline
   6½ million refrigerators
  200 million tons of steel.[1]

So the next time you hear a baby cry, don't let it annoy you. Today's babies are our customers of tomorrow.

To produce for this rapidly growing market, industry will have to increase its capacity and raise its efficiency. It may seem untimely to be talking about expansion, but experts estimate that, in the next ten years alone, business-

[1] "People and Production," *Better Living*, September-October 1960, E. I. du Pont de Nemours and Company.

men will have to raise $560 billion in new capital to keep our capacity up to the increased demand.[2]

Just raising the capital required will be a tough enough job, but the key point I want to drive home is this: *All this growth—all this potential $750 billion economy—is just that: Potential!* It is not going to drop into our laps. We are going to have to work for it—harder and smarter than at any time in our history.

But no matter how hard we work, we can reach our goal *only* if we provide a business climate favorable to growth in the American tradition. Make no mistake. The kind of growth and the means used to achieve it are crucial considerations. Artificially induced growth is not consistent with our political and economic systems. It would weaken rather than strengthen the economy as a whole.

Our big challenge is to encourage sound growth within the private sector of our economy. Under free enterprise, sound growth takes place when we have strong profit incentives which lead individuals and companies to provide more jobs. Perhaps I can best explain what I mean by describing the situation in the steel industry.

Experts estimate that the steel industry will have to spend $12 billion for expansion and modernization between now and 1970 to keep abreast of demand. This is a pretty tough assignment if you remember that the total value of the steel industry was roughly $8 billion only ten years ago.

This same problem is faced by all of our industries. So the question must be asked, "Who is going to provide the needed capital?" If private industry is to provide it, we must assume that it will be profitable for us to do so and that

[2] *The Decade of Incentive*, McCann-Erickson, Inc., p. 3.

the business climate will enourage companies like ours to grow and prosper.

Unfortunately, three big obstacles stand in the way of growth: the persistent problem of inflation, the unrealistic depreciation policies of the federal government, and the high and rising levels of taxation.

I do not have to remind businessmen that inflation is bad. Even the public is learning that inflation raises consumer prices and plays havoc with the family budget. But we have failed to get across to the public and to our employees the fact that *companies have the same trouble with high prices that individuals do.* Here is what we have to contend with when we do our company buying in Republic.

The cost of mill rolls is up 125 per cent—molds are up 65 per cent—iron ore is up 85 per cent—grinding wheels are up 70 per cent—and employment costs have risen 135 per cent since 1948. While all this was going on, output per man-hour increased only 35 per cent.

I certainly sympathize with parents who have to stretch a limited budget over the cost of caring for a growing family. They have to worry about doctor bills and the high cost of maintaining a home.

In a somewhat similar way, we in business management have to worry about the high cost of repairs and new equipment. Let me give you some typical examples. The cost of a major overhaul on some of our blast furnaces is higher today than the original cost of the furnace. A new open hearth shop costs about $64 million compared to an original cost of $10 million for the shop it replaces. In anybody's book, that is inflation!

We can offset these inflated costs somewhat by increasing the efficiency of our productive facilities. For example, we are using oxygen in open hearth furnaces, and several companies are turning to oxygen converters to lower costs. But no matter what we do we are still paying for the years of inflation since World War II.

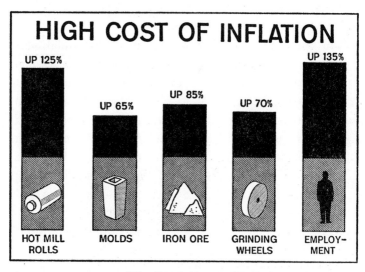

FIG. 3   The High Cost of Inflation

REPUBLIC'S COSTS 1948-1960

Another thing that makes this situation so painful is that we do not have much leeway in our capital budget. When buying equipment we have to buy the best and keep our company at peak efficiency or we cannot compete. This problem, incidentally, is due to get worse as the pace of change increases the need for capital outlays.

Our work is cut out for us. We must keep hammering away until every employee and every voter and every congressman understands why we want to check the wage-push behind inflation, and why efficiency and economy in government—local and state as well as federal—should have the highest priority in the years ahead.

Inflation has made our federal government's depreciation policy unrealistic. Leading economists estimate that replacement costs in American industry are exceeding depreciation allowances by at least $6 billion a year.[3]

In a recent study, Father William Hogan of Fordham University concluded that serious unemployment may result unless something is done about this drain on our capital resources.[4]

The gravity of the problem is apparent when you read in the study that one-third of our plant and equipment is obsolete and that another $60 billion worth will become obsolete by 1970.

Both the National Bureau of Economic Research and the Rand Corporation agree that technological advances have accounted for 90 per cent of the rise in output per man-hour in the United States in modern times. It follows then, that by slowing the rate of improvement our depreciation policy is slowing our rate of economic progress.

It is essential that we solve this depreciation problem now, or it will get progressively worse in the years ahead.

For the same reasons, the tax load on individuals and corporations should be reduced to encourage the new investments needed to promote future growth.

I suppose people get tired of hearing businessmen talk about taxes, but I wonder if they are really aware of the mounting taxes our companies pay each year. In 1960, for example, *Republic's tax bill alone would have built the George Washington Bridge and all its approaches—or even the Pentagon, one of the world's largest buildings.*

The important point is this: inflation, unrealistic de-

[3] *Monthly Bank Letter* of the First National City Bank of New York, September, 1960, p. 7.

[4] Hogan, William T. and Frank T. Koelble, "Economic Depreciation and Employment in the 1960's," *Thought*, Winter 1960.

preciation, and high taxes are making it hard for us to maintain the profitability—the survivability and growability—of our business firms.

MAINTAINING PROFITABILITY

Profit is the incentive for growth. Without it there would be no capitalistic system—no way of attracting the savings of the people for the good of the country. Therefore, as we see it, the maintenance of profitable business operations is another basic imperative that business management faces in the Sixties.

There are, of course, many factors that affect our ability to earn a profit, but I would like to say a few words about the cost-price squeeze and employee attitudes toward profits.

Since 1958, our company has been caught between constantly rising costs and a frozen price structure for our products. Like other companies in our industry, we have experienced stiffer taxes—particularly at the state and local levels—rising transportation charges, increased materials and service costs, and much higher wages and benefits brought on by powerful union pressures.

All of these are important, but the hardest one to do anything about is the high cost of labor. Somehow—by education, by reason, by persuasion—management must bring home to union leaders and union members alike the fact that wages *cannot* be raised every time labor negotiations come around. They must see that even when gains are made in productivity these gains must be shared among labor, stockholders, the company's own capital needs, and the public in the form of cheaper or better products. Some-

14

how, they must come to realize that they defeat their own cause when pay increases exceed gains in efficiency, thereby contributing to inflation and impairing our ability to compete.

Perhaps part of the answer to this problem is better communication with our employees about the role of profits in our economy. We have made some progress in this area, but we must make much more. It may seem strange that we have to do this, because it should be obvious to anyone that when we are making money everyone is better off; and when we are losing money, there is less employment, less income, and less security. But some people have the idea that they are being deprived of something when business makes a profit.

Actually, a profitable company is the most creative of institutions. It provides jobs and opportunities. It assures the community of a payroll and a future. It is the basic source of security for employees and their families. These are the truths we should tell over and over until every employee, every customer, and every voter knows them by heart.

The challenge is clear: we must maintain profitability or there is little likelihood that we can handle the serious competitive challenges which lie ahead.

THE PROBLEM OF DOMESTIC COMPETITION

I turn now to the problem of domestic competition. Vigorous competition is essential to our economy because it helps reconcile our consumer and producer interests with the public interest—and, in a big country like ours, believe me that is quite a job. We have about 67 *million* Americans working together in approximately nine million farms and businesses, and producing the highest standard of living in the world.

But when we look for the person or agency that has the master plan for this enormous national production, we look in vain. No central authority decides what or how much to produce. No law says we have to make steel in Cleveland, or movies in Hollywood, or cheese in Wisconsin.

We leave all such decisions to freedom of choice and a fair shake for everybody in the market place. That is why competition and freedom are two pieces cut from the same cloth.

Competition comes naturally to American businessmen. We like competition. We do not like state control; it hampers national creativity and interferes with sound national growth.

We believe in the kind of competition our forefathers saw when the railroad revolutionized passenger travel and the hauling of mail and freight—not because it ran the stagecoach and the wagon train out of business, but because it made living easier and opened the way for a level of commerce no one had ever seen before.

There have been countless examples of competition in our history and the results have usually been the same. As one product or service supplanted another, new sinews of strength have been added to our country's competitive muscle.

Competition causes some hardships but that is the price of progress. As I see it, competition forces us to be appreciative of our customers, realistic about day-to-day operations, and respectful of competitors. Second-rate managements can hide behind rising prices or higher operating volumes, but the chips are down when we have keen competition. America was not built or kept strong by men of little competitive faith. It was built by men of confidence who were willing to risk their fortunes and their lives for what they wanted. Our American system was conceived in this spirit. It can survive in no other.

We are in the midst of a great competitive struggle both at home and abroad. In a sense, we are being asked to put it on the line as a management and as a nation. It is imperative, therefore, that we take a close look at the things we must do to compete effectively.

No one is more conscious than I am of the actual and potential competition that exists between steel and other materials in the metal market. There is an ever-increasing number of cases where rival materials have invaded traditional steel markets. Steel faces competition in products as diverse as building panels, containers, furniture, auto parts, and mobile homes. And the list is long and growing.

We in the steel industry are conscious of these challenges, and we are not sitting still. But to get a balanced perspective of our problem, we must look at the metal market as a whole.

The fact is that most non-ferrous producers are operating far below capacity and at comparatively weakened prices. When you add up the entire domestic output of all non-ferrous metals in 1960—including aluminum, copper, and all the rest—you get less than four million tons. During the same period, steel production was about 100 million tons, even though the industry operated at far less than capacity. So, although we are taking our competition seriously, we believe steel is and will remain the metallic backbone of our economy.

On the other hand, we are not telling ourselves any fairy tales. Other metals *are* concentrating on some of our most profitable product areas. Designers *are* displacing steel with air as they turn to lighter, more compact designs. Many of our competitors *do* look to steel's present markets for their future growth. We are taking, therefore, the most aggressive steps in our history to improve our processes, our products, our efficiency, and our marketing.

To illustrate, let us take a quick look at the current trends in steel industry research and marketing.

Until recently, iron and steel were produced in facilities and by processes similar to those used a hundred years ago. The open hearth furnace, for example, which is still the mainstay of our steel production, goes back to 1858 in terms of discovery.

This lack of technological innovation was largely due to the fact that there was no compelling *need* for change. What the country needed was more conventional steel, and the steel industry served its customers best by turning out more of the same during periods of peace and war.

After World War II, however, there were dramatic changes throughout American industry. The expanding frontiers of research led the nation into a new industrial era, paced by striking advances in electronics, metallurgy, and physics. New materials and new processes became commonplace—and whenever our economic appetite showed signs of waning, it was stimulated by a wide variety of new products and processes.

The steel industry has done its share in this technological revolution, and its role is growing. At Republic Steel we have greatly expanded our effort, all the way from basic research to product development. We are now probing for the essential secrets of metal structure; we are seeking the ultimate refinement in our machines and processes; we are looking through our customers' eyes at products and services; and we are setting hard-to-reach goals for efficiency and quality—goals that can be achieved only through major advances in controls and testing. Even so, Republic's research is just a fraction of what is going on today in the steel industry. What it all amounts to is a forced march by most steel companies in the direction of greater research and technical progress. This situation is typical of all American industry.

The increased emphasis on research and development in this country has been accompanied by striking advances in design and styling—two factors that tend to make consumers long for things they have never had. As a result, we have moved irresistibly toward the light, the strong, the colorful, and the esthetic—and we have made practically a fetish of the new and the different.

But all the research and design in the world and even a host of new products would not do the job for us if marketing and sales failed to keep pace. At this point I would be less than candid if I did not say that some people feel that the steel industry fell down in this area after World War II—that we developed the habit of being mere order *takers* rather than order *makers*.

Whether they are right or wrong, one thing is clear: the easy sell is over, and the time for the smart sell is here. We have learned that we must improve our market impact if we want to stay in business.

No industry can sit still and rest on its laurels. It must improve. It must change. It must adapt to the consumer or it dies. Success in the decade ahead will come to the imaginative, the risk takers, the developers, the flexible, and the aggressive.

We have faced up to this fact at Republic Steel. Here are some of the things we are doing about it.

First, we are intensifying our training program for our sales staff. We have developed an Order Makers Institute to help train the personnel of companies that distribute our products.

Second, we are placing heavy emphasis on customer service, for we feel it may be the decisive factor in the Sixties.

Third, we are turning more and more to electronic equipment in scheduling customer orders, in market research, in production processing, and in inventory control.

As an industry we have adopted the STEELMARK so people will readily know that many of the products they buy are made of steel. By the use of this mark we are going right to the consumer to increase the use and to broaden the market for steel.

We are going to sell smart, and we are going to sell close to the customer. We are going to know him like a brother, and like a brother we are going to be there when he needs us.

More and more we will be dealing with our customers as people—always trying to find new ways to make our laboratories and production lines the servants of mankind.

THE CHALLENGE OF PEOPLE

A company's success in the Sixties will depend on many factors, but an important one will certainly be people. After all, a company is far more than brick and mortar. Money is important, and so are materials and technology. But the motivating factor, the guiding factor is people—always people.

People can be our greatest asset or our biggest problem. They can guarantee our survival or bring about our ruin.

They can understand and cooperate or misunderstand and destroy.

So the future of our companies depends to a very considerable degree upon our employees—their skills, their abilities, and their ideas. Can we develop them? Can we win their loyalty and dedication? I think we can, and I will discuss later the things we must do to improve our human resources.

How well we do in the Sixties will depend in large part on how seriously we dedicate ourselves to outstanding performance in all of these important problem areas at home—the ideological challenge, the population explosion, the problem of economic growth, the problem of maintaining profitability, the problem of domestic competition, and the challenge of people.

The problems are great, and the challenges are humbling to all of us. But the opportunities *are greater than at any time in our history*. If we dedicate ourselves to the task ahead we can still make the coming decade the "Soaring Sixties" we all foresaw at the end of the Fifties. And at Republic Steel we intend to try.

THE PROBLEMS ABROAD

Let us turn, now, to the international scene where, again, we face problems of great magnitude. New alliances are forming, old ideas are being discarded, isolationism is dying, and in its place a new spirit of global competition is emerging.

There was a time when a businessman had to think only of his company and his community. The domestic market was profitable and comparatively uncomplicated, and it almost completely dominated business planning.

But today's businessman is directly affected by what happens abroad. That fact is being driven home to him by the rising pressure of foreign competition and the growing potential of world markets.

In a broader sense every citizen is beginning to realize that we live in a world of great tension and compression. Politically, we live in a divided world dominated by the split atom. Culturally, we are seeing the turbulent masses of the world stirring with rampant nationalism that is sweeping across entire continents. Economically, we are experiencing an aggressive invasion of our domestic and foreign markets by friend and foe alike. Technologically, we live in a world compressed in space and time. Today jets fly to Europe in six hours. Before the decade is out, we may have landed on the moon.

In a world seething with change, we businessmen can no longer be isolationists. We must become interested in foreign affairs and international trade. I say "must" because of our need for resources, for markets, and for friends.

Frankly, I feel humble as I start reviewing some of the foreign problems that confront us in the years ahead. I am a businessman, not an authority on world affairs or international trade. But you may be interested in hearing some of the conclusions we have come to at Republic Steel. Our industry has special problems, of course, but our international problems are similar to those confronting American business in general.

OUR NATURAL RESOURCES PROBLEM

The Fifties were a period of unprecedented growth for the United States, but they also marked the point in our history when we became a have-not nation in many natural resources.

There are about seventy-seven critical and strategic materials upon which our country depends. Some of them are not found in commercial quantities within our borders, while others are in short supply. Therefore we are importing them in growing quantities from abroad. In some instances we have been able to relieve the shortage by mechanically upgrading low-grade domestic ores, but the cost of this operation is usually high. That is why foreign supplies of high grade ores are so important to our domestic industries.

In 1959 more than half of our copper was imported, with Chile supplying about 44 per cent. Most of our manganese came from abroad. Practically all of our nickel came from Canada. Bauxite, the basic ore from which aluminum is reduced, came largely from Jamaica, Surinam, and the Dominican Republic.

I could mention other examples, but these are sufficient to make this key point: we are dependent today upon foreign sources for much of the raw material that feeds our mass production industries—and the situation will get worse as our population increases and our economy expands.

Our experience in the steel industry is typical of what other industries are running into as far as raw materials are concerned.

America has always been the largest producer of iron ore. Even as late as 1950 we produced over 40 per cent of the world's output.[5] But our role as the arsenal of democracy in two world wars coupled with the tremendous rise in steel consumption for civilian uses made a huge dent in our domestic iron ore reserves.

The signs of trouble could not be ignored after World War II. There was a growing interest in the exploration and development of foreign sources, as well as in new methods for upgrading domestic ores that were low in iron content. During the Fifties, major iron ore bodies were developed in Canada, South America, and Africa.

Republic Steel had a hand in opening up the great new iron ore deposits of Labrador and in developing a body of high quality ore in Liberia. We also joined Armco Steel Corporation to mine and process magnetic taconite—a low-grade, iron-bearing rock found in tremendous quantities in northern Minnesota.

All of these developments have cost a considerable amount of money. American iron and steel companies have invested more than $2 billion in iron ore projects during the last ten years, and about half of this money has gone into projects outside the country.

[5] *Annual Statistical Report*, American Iron and Steel Institute, 1959, pp. 124-127.

What is our raw materials situation in the steel industry today? Well, for the Sixties the answer is definitely good. Studies indicate, however, that high-grade iron ore will become increasingly scarce in the long-range future. World demand for steel is expected to double in the next fifteen years, and as the iron content of ore goes down the problem will be intensified.[6]

In other industries the situation ranges from good to critical. But competition for raw materials throughout the world will increase greatly in the years ahead as more countries build or expand their manufacturing facilities and absorb more of the output of their own mines. We can also expect heavier competition from other have-not industrial nations such as Japan.

A careful review of our raw materials picture reveals four points that should be remembered.

First, we are becoming increasingly dependent upon foreign sources for iron ore, copper, bauxite, and other critical and strategic materials.

Second, in some cases this dependence can be lessened by the mechanical upgrading of low-grade domestic ores, but such projects require large capital expenditures.

Third, the low-cost reserves of these materials are frequently found in the underdeveloped countries of the world where leadership is lacking and the political climate is unstable.

Fourth, as raw materials become scarcer they may become a cause of international tension, particularly—as we shall see later—in our dealings with the underdeveloped countries and with Soviet Russia.

[6] *Long Term Trends and Problems of the European Steel Industry*, Secretariat of the Economic Commission for Europe, United Nations, 1959, p. 171.

We will have to increase our efforts in three directions: locating and developing new foreign sources of ore; finding better ways to utilize low-grade domestic ores; and finding substitute materials for those in short supply.

Because of their present importance as sources of raw materials and because of their potential importance as markets for goods in the future, let us turn at this point to the underdeveloped nations which are so much in the world spotlight today.

THE UNDERDEVELOPED AREAS OF THE WORLD

These underdeveloped areas have been there all along— South America, Asia, and the explosive continent of Africa. But how many businessmen understand their real potential—except, perhaps, as sources of raw materials or as trouble spots on the political map of the world?

But understand them we must. Their bulging populations, their intense nationalism, their rising expectations, and their drive toward industrialization will not be denied. Together, these continents constitute another serious foreign problem for the decade.

Today, four out of every five children born are citizens of underdeveloped nations. The only curve that is rising faster than their population curve is their expectations curve— their yearning for a better life and a higher standard of living.

The United States has helped raise these expectations with its movies and mail order catalogues. We have made these people conscious of the great differences between our way of life and theirs; and, having seen the vision, they will

26

be satisfied with nothing less. But their production and purchasing power are lagging far behind.

In America, the gap between expectations and production is comparatively small. Throughout the free world the situation is improving with each passing year. But in the underdeveloped countries, conditions are different.

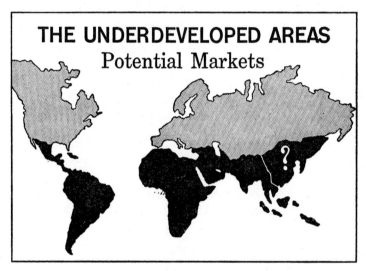

FIG. 4   The Underdeveloped Areas

The degree of poverty in these countries is not realized by most people, even though they read daily reports of political and economic unrest all around the world. In 1958, for example, the United States had about 233 people per square mile of arable land compared with 1,638 for China. An economic study made in 1957 showed our Gross National Product at $2,570 per person compared with an estimated $371 for Spain, $69 for Bolivia, and $47 for Ethiopia.[7]

[7] *The United States Economy and the Mutual Security Program*, Department of State, April 1959, p. 59.

27

Overcrowding, with too many people on too little land; poverty, with too little income to satisfy needs; lack of capital, with little prospect for home-financed industrial expansion—these are some of the causes behind the world's unrest.

India, for example, has a population of more than 400 million, but a per capita output equal to only 2 per cent of ours.[8] In spite of her huge resources, the average Indian's diet is far below the minimum requirement for good nutrition.

Directly south of us are twenty-one Latin American countries with a population of 200 million, a total land area of almost 8 million square miles, and tremendous natural resources awaiting development. These countries could have an economic growth comparable to ours, but their per capita income is extremely low.

Nonetheless, the potential of the region can be seen by what has happened to Mexico. Industrial production in Mexico has climbed 59 per cent since 1953.[9] By 1970, per capita output is expected to reach $500.[10]

This is still low by our standards, but measured against their past poverty it represents real progress. If other Latin American countries can make similar progress we will have a rich, new market south of the border—an entirely new horizon for tomorrow's export business.

It is no exaggeration to say that *a major part of tomorrow's markets lies in the underdeveloped countries of the world*—and as of now they have hardly been tapped.

We must bear in mind, however, that many of these countries are just coming of age, so to speak. They lack a

[8] *The Decade of Incentive*, p. 9.
[9] *Monthly Bulletin of Statistics*, United Nations, January 1961.
[10] *The Decade of Incentive*, p. 6.

stable middle class; they are thin in responsible leadership, and many of them have no experience in self-government. An extreme nationalism may be combined with these short-comings—or, what is worse, a pseudo-nationalism generated by subversive elements.

Bureaucratic regulation, confiscation, and nationalization are clear and present dangers even in reasonably well-developed countries. A striking example is Cuba, which in 1960 alone took over almost one billion dollars in American properties.

I mention this to indicate the real problems we face if we pursue the world's markets with vigor and determination. We must convince these countries that friendliness to America and American businessmen will be good business for them in this decade and beyond.

But business cannot do the job alone. Foreign relations are too involved with power politics and the looming threat of war. The Federal government, through its diplomatic channels, must help protect American investments from arbitrary seizure. We must be good neighbors ourselves, but we should expect neighborly treatment in return.

This problem of the underdeveloped countries is complicated by the fact that if we do not help them develop their vast market potential Soviet Russia undoubtedly will, thereby staking out a claim on markets that could be ours.

THE GROWING STRUGGLE WITH COMMUNISM

This brings us to what may prove to be the most critical problem we face abroad: the growing struggle with communism as an economic as well as political force.

During the past twenty-five years the Communists have

taken over fifteen nations which once were free. They have expanded at the rate of almost 538 square miles a day, and now occupy about 25 per cent of the land surface of the globe. They control almost 40 per cent of the world's people and dominate their markets.[11]

Is the situation any better today? A look around the world supplies the answer. Algeria, Japan, Cuba, the Congo, Ghana, Laos, Vietnam—all show the results of steady Communist pressure.

This, then, is the enemy we are up against—an enemy who is waging economic as well as political war. Whether we like it or not, we must fight this war with world markets as the battlefield, and machines, raw materials, and manpower as the assault weapons.

The immediate struggle is going on in the underdeveloped countries because their low living standards make them ripe for economic and political conquest.

Africa is far away, so it is easy to minimize what is happening there. But in terms of the future, we cannot afford to see Africa drift into the Communist orbit or Cuba permanently lost to Communist domination. As Cuba has gone, other Latin American countries may go, thus making South America the soft underbelly of the Western Hemisphere and closing to American businessmen a great area of resources and markets.

The underdeveloped nations are not the only danger spots. Russia has opened a second front by bringing her economic war to the nations of the Western Alliance. Her campaign has just started, but we are already learning that dumping can be a powerful weapon.

Thus far it has been used in only a few key materials such as oil, aluminum, and wool. But if Russia can keep

[11] *The Economic Almanac*, National Industrial Conference Board, 1960, pp. 18-19.

her people at a comparatively low standard of living, she can plow back more of her total wealth into the tools of production and continue to unsettle the world market.

During the next ten years, she could become a real adversary in international trade because she can ignore market costs in the short run to achieve long-term political gains.

We know that Russia is strong and that her strength is growing. Some experts believe that by 1970 the Soviet Union will probably increase its total output by 86 per cent while ours will only go up about 49 per cent.[12] True, they start from a lower base, but their present rate of growth is impressive.

We should take their output figures with a grain of salt, *but we cannot ignore them.* The Russians are making major gains in steelmaking, machine tools, and construction. They are investing heavily in automation and electronic equipment.

Republic's former chief metallurgist visited Russia shortly before his death and he found some of their blast furnaces superior to ours. Other visiting experts have found so many examples of outstanding progress that it would be sheer folly to take them lightly or to ignore their potential.

Through an astonishing feat of prophecy 125 years ago, Alexis de Tocqueville in his *Democracy in America* summed up our present dilemma neatly:

There are . . . two great nations in the world which seem to tend towards the same end, although they started from different points: I allude to the Russians and the Americans. Both of them have grown up unnoticed; and whilst the attention of mankind was directed elsewhere, they have suddenly assumed a most prominent place amongst the nations . . .
. . . The American struggles against the natural obstacles which oppose him; the adversaries of the Russian are men; the former

[12] "Sharp Gains Seen in Soviet Output," *New York Times,* June 23, 1960.

combats the wilderness and savage life; the latter, civilization with all its weapons and its arts: the conquests of the one are therefore gained by the ploughshare; those of the other by the sword. The Anglo-American relies upon personal interest to accomplish his ends, and gives free scope to the unguided exertions and common-sense of the citizens; the Russian centres all the authority of society in a single arm: the principal instrument of the former is freedom; of the latter servitude. Their starting-point is different, and their courses are not the same; yet each of them seems to be marked out by the will of Heaven to sway the destinies of half the globe.

If de Tocqueville were alive today, I am sure he would be surprised at the profound accuracy of his statement. Everything we do in the international field—be it social, political, cultural, economic, or military—is conditioned today by the rising power of the Soviet Union.

If the Russians mean what they say, and if the scattered examples of their economic aggression are indications of what is to come, we must prepare for competition the like of which we have never seen.

There are practical steps we can take to meet this economic aggression, and I will describe some of them later. But first, I want to discuss another form of competition we face: the increased competition with our allies.

INCREASED ECONOMIC COMPETITION WITH OUR ALLIES

Since World War II, the United States has experienced a spectacular rise in production and living standards. We have had recessions and they have hurt. But looking back, we can see that they were only minor interruptions in the upward surge of our economy.

Now, however, we seem to be in trouble. Our friends and allies are fighting us tooth and nail for markets—quite successfully, I might add—and many of us are embarrassed

by that fact. We should not be embarrassed. Our performance has continued to improve—but theirs has improved
faster. Even if it hurts, this is a healthy situation. It is a
challenge, not a catastrophe.

It seems only a few years ago that the war-ravaged countries of Europe were flat on their backs. The big question
is, how have they bounced back so soon?

Actually, there is nothing mysterious about it. They have
worked in a Herculean way to rebuild their industries. They
have gone without luxuries and plowed back a high percentage of their gains to improve their industrial potential.

But a major factor has been the $74 billion in American
government aid and loans and the $24 billion in private
investments we have made abroad since the war. We have
also made important contributions in production methods
and in technical assistance—all with the deliberate intent
of building up the strength of the Free World.

The result of all of these factors is an astonishing European recovery that is gratifying in a political sense, but
somewhat disturbing economically. It leaves us with two
major problems to solve: first, the problem of balancing
our international payments, and, second, the problem of
meeting the powerful competition we have helped create.

The balance of payments problem is largely the result of
our huge foreign aid program. Our net income from ex-
ports and foreign investments offset this tremendous
drain during the late Forties, but, since 1950, despite a
favorable trade balance, our balance of payments has been
written in red ink. During the last three years alone the
outflow of funds has exceeded the inflow by about $11
billion.

Clearly something must be done—but what? We could,
I suppose, cut off foreign aid completely, return to a policy

of high tariffs, and limit our freedom to invest abroad. But in the long run these are not practical solutions for a great nation such as ours.

It seems to me that the American people have three basic alternatives, after providing for necessary defense and aid programs: we can cut non-essential government expenditures; we can raise our income from international trade, or we can do both.

This third alternative gives us flexibility. It permits us to invest abroad, to conduct trade in an open and competitive way, and to carry on aid programs which strengthen the Western World. And, equally important, this alternative is possible.

One thing is clear, however. To raise our income from international trade we must improve our competitive edge and make a greater impact in the world's markets. This will not be easy. Our recent experience in the steel industry shows how tough the competition will be as foreign production expands and improves. In certain wire, pipe, and bar products, for example, foreign competitors have been able to pay ocean freight and still undercut us in price in our home markets.

We can hold our own and even improve our position if we move with intelligence and vigor. As I see it, there are nine steps we can take to increase our competitive strength during the coming decade.

First, *We Can Improve Our Customer Service*

With our domestic customers, we have the built-in advantages of service, speed of delivery, and technical assistance that help offset the lower costs of foreign producers competing in our home markets. We should make sure that this same service is extended to our foreign customers as well.

Second, *We Can Improve Quality and Raise Efficiency*

To compete effectively abroad, we must raise the quality of our products and improve the over-all efficiency of our operations. At Republic we are in the middle of a $375 million capital spending program to do just this. This trend is typical of all progressive American companies and must continue in the future.

1162650

Third, *We Can Intensify Our Research Effort*

We must look to research to develop better processes and to create the new and improved products needed to protect old markets and to gain new ones.

Private spending for research and development reached an estimated $12.5 billion in 1960 and will probably double by 1970.[13] I doubt that our foreign competitors can match this effort; if they cannot, we will gradually move ahead of them in efficiency and in the variety and quality of our products.

Fourth, *We Must Reduce the Gap Between Employment Costs and Productivity*

Somehow, every worker in America must come to see the danger in the wage gap that exists between our workers and those abroad. In 1959, average employment costs in our domestic steel industry were $3.80 an hour. This compared with $1.13 in West Germany, $.91 in France, $.96

[13] *The Outlook for Expenditures on Research and Development during the Next Decade*, McGraw-Hill, Inc., Department of Economics, April 1, 1960.

in the Netherlands, and $.55 in Japan. Obviously, such a wide difference in employment costs gives foreign companies a decided advantage.

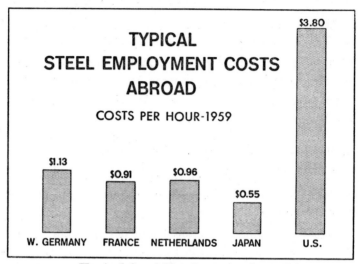

FIG. 5 Typical Steel Employment Costs Abroad

In the past we were able to cope with this handicap because we had better tools and production methods. But today many of our foreign competitors have plants and facilities as modern and as well-managed as ours.

Moreover, their lower construction and equipment costs permit them to build new capacity for considerably less money than it takes to do the same job here. So besides their lower operating costs, they have the advantage of lower capital costs.

These cost differences will become increasingly critical as foreign expansion programs are completed. For example, in 1958 the countries of the European Coal and Steel Community had 75 million net tons of steel ingot capacity. But by 1965 they will have a capacity of about 98 million tons[14]—a gain of 23 million tons of productive, ultra-modern steelmaking capacity in just seven years.

This leaves us no alternative. We must call a halt to spiraling employment costs and raise our productivity if we want to remain competitive in the world's markets.

Fifth, *We Can Overhaul Our Outmoded Depreciation Policy*

I have pointed out that our obsolete depreciation policy is a big obstacle to our progress at home. It is an even bigger obstacle to our ability to compete abroad.

Foreign countries permit a much faster write-off of new equipment than we do. Some permit a revaluation of capital assets when inflation increases replacement costs. Others simply grant deductions greater than the original cost. In many countries, allowances equal to half the total cost are permitted in the first year.[15]

The lesson is unmistakable. To compete abroad, we must retain and increase our historic leadership in technology. To do this we must be able to replace facilities as soon as they become inefficient or obsolete. This throws the spotlight squarely on our government's outmoded depreciation policy.

Sixth, *We Can Be More Aggressive in Marketing and Sales*

Perhaps the quickest and most effective way to improve our competitive edge is to apply to foreign markets the same "smart sell" methods we use in our domestic markets. At home, you might say that the gap between our sales problems and their solution is only two or three feet—the

[14] *European Steel Market in 1959*, Secretariat of the Economic Commission for Europe, United Nations, 1960, pp. 79 and 85.
[15] *Monthly Bank Letter* of the First National City Bank of New York, September, 1960, p. 7.

distance from the back of the sales counter to our customers. This personal touch becomes complicated, however, when the customer is two or three thousand miles away.

One solution, of course, is to go where the customers are. American firms are establishing themselves abroad at a much faster rate than ever before. For a measure of the scope of these operations, the total cumulative value of American private long-term investments abroad climbed from $17.5 billion in 1950 to an estimated $45 billion in 1960.[16] This trend is likely to accelerate in many industries as companies are pulled by growing markets and low costs abroad and pushed by high taxes and high costs at home.

This is only a limited answer to the over-all problem. It will be much better if we can strengthen our domestic industry and increase the export of American goods. We can expect a battle, but the rewards are worth it. The experience of Standard of New Jersey, H. J. Heinz, Colgate-Palmolive, and National Cash Register—to name only a few companies—illustrates the growing potential of foreign markets.

Yet we must remember that foreign countries have their own particular needs, customs, and standards. If we want their business we must learn to talk their language in the broadest sense of the word. We must learn to be likeable in Madrid and Rotterdam as well as in Detroit and Philadelphia.

Furthermore, we will have to pay more than lip service to the *goals* of these people in foreign lands. Does our presence have a constructive effect on their society? Are we making friends for democracy and for free enterprise?

Some progress has been made in recent years in training

[16] U.S. Department of Commerce.

executives who may be responsible for foreign business relations. For example, the Business Council for International Understanding now sponsors a special training program for businessmen at The American University in Washington, D. C. The purpose of the program is to create a better understanding of the institutions and viewpoints of the United States and of the other countries where executives may be stationed.

Seventh, *We Can Continue to Work for a Strong Anti-Inflation Policy at Home*

Inflation weakens us abroad just as surely as it weakens us at home. By fighting for government efficiency and fighting against deficit spending and inflation, we can prevent the deterioration of the dollar and stop the drain on our gold reserves.

Eighth, *We Can Act to Remove the Present Trade Restrictions on American Goods*

On the whole, the United States freely permits imports, even though the countries shipping to us may have stiff tariffs or quotas on American products entering their countries. This situation has improved in recent years, and progress is continuing.

The United States, along with twenty-three other countries, is participating in the Geneva meetings of GATT, the General Agreement on Tariffs and Trade. These meetings are concerned with negotiations for an exchange of new tariff concessions on a multitude of different American goods involved in world trade. Most of the important items we import or export are included in the discussions.

Through such meetings—and by every other appropriate means—our government should press for fair treatment of all American goods in the world's markets.

Developments in the European Economic Community and the European Free Trade Area are also promising. The Inner Six and the Outer Seven, as they are called, represent the striving of our European allies for free trade between the European nations. There is a growing probability that these two groups will unite to form an even stronger economic union. This is good, provided it does not lead to a new wall of trade restrictions against the United States and the rest of the free world.

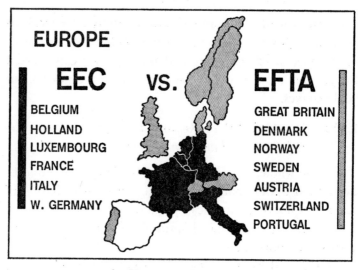

FIG. 6 Europe: EEC vs. EFTA

A step in the right direction was made recently when the United States and Canada joined eighteen European nations in setting up the Organization for Economic Cooperation and Development. One of its principal aims is to stimulate multilateral, nondiscriminatory trade throughout the world.

A second step was the formation of the Latin American

Free Trade Association. LAFTA has now been ratified by Argentina, Chile, Paraguay, and Mexico—and Brazil, Peru, and Uruguay are expected to join at an early date. Actual tariff bargaining is expected to get under way early in the spring of 1961. If these two developments succeed, the competitive position of American goods in world markets may be definitely improved.

Ninth, *We Should Make a Critical Appraisal of Our Foreign Aid Programs*

Even if we make a substantial improvement in our *balance of trade,* however, we may still wind up with an adverse *balance of payments* because of our heavy foreign aid programs. Foreign economic aid is still running at the rate of $3 billion a year. We are asking our allies to share these costs, and we are hopeful that they will cooperate. Thanks to our help in the past, they are now economically strong and are able to stand on their own feet. We believe they should be willing to bear some of the burden of helping the backward nations, thereby reducing the drain on our own economy.

Foreign aid spending should be coordinated with the purchase of American goods. In the past, we have bought products manufactured abroad for use in our aid programs. Where price and quality are reasonably competitive, products made in America should be shipped. Likewise, when purchasing for our armed forces overseas, we should see that American supplies are bought whenever practical.

These steps will help reduce the drain on American funds and help improve our balance of payments.

None of these solutions will be easy to carry out. There is no magic formula that will guarantee success in foreign trade or safeguard our interests abroad. We must examine

41

our record in human relations, business economics, marketing, research, and technology. We must profit by our mistakes, make sure that our plans for the future are practical, and make the best possible use of our resources.

We must also look within. We must renew the faith, moral courage, and devotion to principle which have always been a part of the American tradition. If our faith is strong, our courage high, and our plans practical, we need have no fear of the future. We will prosper and we will earn anew our place of respect and leadership in the world.

BUSINESS STRATEGY FOR A PROSPEROUS DECADE

As we look ahead into the problems and challenges of the Sixties it becomes increasingly clear that this period will be a decade of decision. Key decisions will have to be made in research, in marketing and sales, in natural resources development, in production methods, in communications, and in finance. On top of that, the decisions we make will be conditioned by the political climate that prevails at the domestic and international levels. In the face of rising pressures at home and abroad, we are going to have to make more decisions faster and better than ever.

MANAGEMENT

Decision-making is management's job. No one can do it for us. More than ever before, we will need managers with exceptional combinations of personality, skills, and moral courage. An important key to a prosperous decade, therefore, will be our ability to locate and develop enough of the right kind of management personnel to meet our needs.

Trace with me the differences in tomorrow's management problems from those ten years ago and you will see why we need a competent managerial group in this country.

In the post-war period, the emphasis was on production

—getting out more of the product to meet a pent-up consumer demand. Tomorrow, the emphasis will be on developing the mass markets required by our expanding productive capacity. If the last decade was production-oriented, this one must be research-oriented, market-minded, cost-conscious, finance-wise, and people-sensitive.

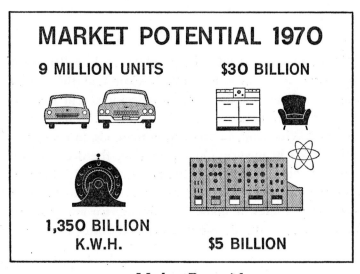

MARKET POTENTIAL 1970

9 MILLION UNITS   **$30 BILLION**

1,350 BILLION K.W.H.   **$5 BILLION**

FIG. 7   Market Potential 1970

During the Fifties we made heavy capital commitments, but we were generally assured of success because we were turning out goods and services for relatively standard markets.

In the Sixties, heavy capital commitments will have to be made, also, but on a much more speculative basis. They will be made to meet potential as well as current competition, and they will involve much greater risk. They will be made to develop and produce new products and materials with less certainty of realizing a profit. They will be made to provide future reserves of raw materials, but with the possibility of confiscation as a serious threat in some foreign areas. In short, capital commitments during the Sixties will be made with far greater risk and will require more personal judgment and a high degree of courage.

During the Fifties, production methods were reasonably standardized. For the most part raising efficiency meant doing our regular jobs better. In other words, efficiency was an evolving process.

The Sixties will place a premium on the seven league boot kind of improvement which leapfrogs the conventional and strives for the breakthrough into new methods and new technology. Process will replace process and product will replace product—as *revolutionary* rather than *evolutionary* changes go into effect. We see it today in the steel industry which is moving simultaneously toward oxygen equipment, direct reduction methods, electronic data processing and computer control, and which seems on the verge of metallurgical breakthroughs in the product area.

Combine all of these things we have discussed—changing markets, the revolution in production methods, increased capital requirements, new and different personnel requirements, the complexity of government regulations and control, foreign as well as domestic problems—and you have operating conditions that demand hard-hitting and versatile decision-makers in the field of management.

The management man of the future must have the moral courage to make momentous decisions often based on a confusing array of facts. He will need creativity and innovation as well as caution. He will have to be flexible in the face of changing situations, using past experience when he feels it applies but throwing it overboard whenever circumstances require that he do so.

Such men are not easy to find. We must make a continuing search throughout every department of our companies for the high-quality few. When we find them, we must develop their potential to the utmost. It will be expensive; it will be time consuming; but it will be indeed a seven league step toward a prosperous decade.

OUR EMPLOYEES

Let us now turn to those employees below the management level—the second big group of people through whom our problems can be solved.

Although tomorrow's technology will give us greater mastery over our physical environment, it will create unprecedented problems in human training and adaptability. Contrary to popular opinion, human skills and resources will become more important—not less—as we move into the future.

The replacement of hand skills by brain power will accelerate. Each new breakthrough in science, each new advance in technology will place new and exacting demands on our employees. Many jobs will become more complex as machines take over the lesser skills now performed by unskilled workers. In many instances we will restore to the employee the sense of responsibility and personal pride in his job that in some ways were lacking in the mass production era.

There will be an accelerating trend from the blue-collar worker to the white-collar worker—and, I might add, to the white-smock worker. An even more marked change will be the rise of the trained technician, engineer, and scientist.

The distinctive feature of these new employees will not

be a particular skill that remains useful over their lifetime, but rather a fund of knowledge that can be adapted to a variety of changing problems.

This trend is evident even in routine maintenance jobs. For example, our electrical maintenance on modern continuous equipment requires more than an ability to splice wires or to change fuses. It now demands a knowledge of electrical circuits and an understanding of electrical theory.

As job requirements rise, it becomes increasingly clear that we are going to run into trouble whenever our employees:

CAN'T DO
DON'T KNOW
DON'T CARE

When a worker CAN'T DO his job well, he lacks confidence; he works in an unsafe way and he works unproductively. As our production processes become more complicated, we have no choice. We must do a better job of employee training.

At Republic Steel we are meeting this training problem in several ways. We now have complete training facilities for upgrading the operating skills of our production and maintenance workers. We have a supervisory development program that covers important knowledge areas and key supervisory skills. And, looking further to the future, we are making it possible for the sons and daughters of our employees to get vocational counselling, free of charge, at special testing centers located in our plant communities.

We believe these steps will help us develop the present and future potential of our plant community labor force and assure a reservoir of qualified people who CAN DO their jobs effectively.

If our employees DON'T KNOW what is going on, they will not be able to help us carry out our long-term goals or understand the effects of their actions on our company performance.

For example, how many employees know the relationship of profits to jobs and job security? Of productivity to wages? To our standard of living? How many understand the relationship of dividends to a company's ability to raise equity capital?

The solution to this DON'T KNOW problem is a continuous program of education and communication. Our employees must know what is going on—not occasionally but day in and day out throughout the year.

At this point I would like to mention four key ideas which we must get across to every employee if we want our companies to prosper in the years ahead.

First, our employees must realize that capital equipment alone is not the answer to our problems. We need more and better machines, and plenty of them. But even more, we need able people who will dedicate themselves to their jobs in mind and spirit as well as in body.

Second, they must come to see that the basic growth of our country depends on the process of saving and investing, on setting aside the seed corn needed for replacement and future expansion.

Third, they must accept the fact that growth and progress mean change, and that change upsets the status quo in bringing about a forward surge. As we move toward a service economy, the character of the labor force itself will change and many adjustments in personal skills will be needed.

Finally, our employees must realize that *our companies are not invulnerable*—that we can remain in business only as long as we meet the basic conditions of survival: new and better products, low cost, high quality, competitive prices, and adequate profits. In a competitive world, inefficient companies simply cannot survive.

We now come to the DON'T CARE attitude. If our employees DON'T CARE, they will not be willing to assume the kind of responsibility their future jobs will require.

A large part of this DON'T CARE attitude is the result of poor communication. It also develops when we forget that all employees are members of the corporate family.

We should never assume that the word "employee" is synonymous with "member of the union." We must look behind the union organization to the individual. All employees want about the same things. Each wants credit for a job well done. He wants a fair consideration of his potential and an equal chance for promotion. He wants a reasonable degree of security for himself and his family. The more convinced he is that the company is fulfilling these desires the more willing he is to dedicate himself to the company's long-term interest.

We should periodically take the temperature of our organization and correct the points of irritation within our control. Definitely, we must provide our employees with a safe place to work, with opportunities for development and advancement, and with full information about impending changes which will affect their status. They will be far less resistant to change if we give them a chance to adapt, to retrain, or to relocate if necessary.

We must also be on the lookout for creative talent wherever it may appear in our organizations. It is easy to maintain the status quo, to adhere to tradition, to frown upon originality and change. To some managers, the old way is the best way and the good worker is the one who does what he is told—and no more. But this will not be sensible strategy in the Sixties. In this era of science and technology, the new way deserves a fair hearing since it may well prove to be the best way in the long run.

Finally, we may have to reconsider the relative importance of our staff services. The trend today is toward three equally important groups within our companies: sales, production, and staff services. In the past, staff services were intended merely to advise and assist the line organizations. Today they are growing in importance. In the near future they may determine the very survival and success of our companies by their ability to develop markets, to create new products, to engineer our way out of difficulties, to cut red tape, or to reduce legal liabilities.

Because of this fact we need to re-examine our present administrative ideas about engineering, marketing, accounting, and research personnel. Unless we understand them and appreciate their contributions they may become the spawning ground for a new crop of employee problems.

I wish I could tell you that we at Republic Steel have come up with definite solutions in these broad areas of CAN'T DO, DON'T KNOW, and DON'T CARE—but that would not be true. We have made some real progress, however, and we intend to make more.

But it is evident from what I have said that we think a company's human resources are its most important asset. That is why, in addition to our training programs, we are making a continuing human resources study of all of our supervisory personnel, cataloguing the individual's education and present skills, and making a determined effort to discover his over-all potential. We believe this inventory

50

will help us locate, develop, and use more effectively the human resources within our company.

This emphasis on the human factor in the Sixties will place a heavy burden on those engaged in personnel administration. Not too long ago personnel work was considered a routine function concerned largely with recruiting employees and maintaining records. But that situation is changing, and the modern trend is toward a higher-level personnel function—one that looks ahead to the long-term problems of a company and plans the best possible use of its human resources.

There is a limit, however, to what a company can do with its human resources. A large part of the problem starts with the schools, and we cannot talk intelligently about plans for a prosperous future without saying something about education.

BUSINESS AND EDUCATION

It is easy to be complacent about our educational system. After all, the people who have graduated from this system have built the most productive economy the world has ever seen. We have broken the grip of poverty, and our people enjoy a standard of living without parallel in any age or in any country on earth. We are on top of the heap. We would not be there if we had seriously neglected the job of education.

But a closer look at our educational system reveals some disturbing flaws in an otherwise favorable picture. Of our adult population, about 45 per cent have finished high school. Less than 8 per cent have graduated from college. Even more disturbing, 38 per cent never advanced beyond the eighth grade. We have improved in recent years, but even today only about 65 per cent of our young people are graduating from high school,[17] while 10 per cent never go beyond the eighth grade.[18] This is a tragic waste of human potential.

A good basic education and some specialized training are becoming increasingly important. The biggest percentage of unemployment today is found among those workers who lack knowledge or skill or who are unwilling to retrain or upgrade their potential.

Unfortunately, this problem is going to get worse rather than better. For example, about 7½ million of the young people who will enter our labor force during the Sixties will have less than a high school education—at the very time when the demand for unskilled labor is dropping and the need for trained personnel is becoming acute.

An equally big educational problem will be the retraining of those people whose skills have become obsolete because of technological advances. This will be particularly serious for workers who have had many years of service with a company only to find that a change in skill is required somewhat late in life. For those over 45, the problem is critical because a full 38 per cent of the unemployed men between the ages of 45 and 64 are in the long-term unemployed category. They represent pressing social problems because they have heavy family responsibilities and many productive years ahead of them.

Unemployment compensation is a poor substitute for employable skills. These skills must be developed if our people are to have the internal security that only a steady

[17] *Health, Education and Welfare Trends,* Department of Health, Education and Welfare, 1960 ed., pp. 60-62.
[18] *Current Population Report,* Series P-20, No. 107, U. S. Department of Commerce, Bureau of the Census, January 16, 1961.

job and better job opportunities can inspire.

Retraining programs in the Sixties will make sense in another way, too. While we may have an oversupply of young, unskilled workers, there are likely to be shortages in the middle-age brackets that make up the backbone of our skilled labor force. If we do not retrain these people the financial load on our employed work force, our companies, and our communities will be heavy indeed.

This is not a job for business alone. We should do our share, but our local communities can help solve the problem by improving their vocational guidance and training programs. Periodic surveys should be carried out in connection with the companies in the area. As new trends develop, training programs should be adjusted to cope with them. This will be particularly important as we move ahead with automation.

For all of these reasons, management must take an even greater interest in education. We businessmen must help make education more universal and see that it is more closely geared to the needs of our times. We can do this in several ways.

First, we can dramatize the role of trained employees in tomorrow's world and encourage our children to regard education as the key to a better and fuller life.

Second, we can clarify the changing needs of business and help keep our schools' curricula up-to-date, with proper emphasis on scientific courses but with equal stress on the sciences of man.

Third, we can take a more active part in school affairs. By so doing we can help to increase teachers' salaries, raise educational standards, provide functional school plants, and bring about a closer cooperation between industry and the school.

I am glad to say that Republic Steel is sincerely trying to meet its obligations to education. We believe we must do so in order to protect the long-range interests of our stockholders, our employees, and our customers.

PUBLIC AND GOVERNMENT RELATIONS

Our concern about education should be extended also to include broader programs for informing the public and all the various levels of government about business policies, problems, and plans.

Our chances for a prosperous decade will be substantially improved if we can generate an over-all business climate that is favorable to economic growth in the American tradition. To do this effectively, we must bear in mind the importance of public opinion and the rapidly growing power of government at all levels of our society.

More than ever before, business is on a stage with a huge public audience watching its every move. This audience has become judge and jury as well as customer, passing its judgment at the ballot box and trying each labor-management conflict in the press and on the airwaves.

In today's world no company can be an island. It is an integral part of the community, the state, and the nation. Therefore we need a long-range program of continuous communication to make sure that the public understands our goals, our business policies, and our positive contributions as well as our problems.

Communication thus becomes a vital part of each manager's job—and by communication we mean a two-way street. We want our managers to listen as well as talk; to speak with deeds as well as words; to take part in civic and community affairs; and to understand our employees' fears as well as their aspirations for better pay and a higher standard of living.

At Republic Steel, in addition to our day-to-day public relations activities, we now have a community advertising program, an active speakers bureau, a program of stockholder communication, an employee magazine, employee newsletters, programs in economic and political education, and a special program for college professors.

This whole field of communication—with employees, plant communities, and the general public—has become so important to us that we have formed a Communication Committee composed of key department heads. This committee meets regularly and plans our company's over-all communication effort.

We have accepted the facts of life in the political arena, too. We believe that business must do two things if we want to prosper in the years ahead:

First, we must fight to preserve freedom of action and market competition in that part of our economy which is still free and competitive.

Second, we must fight with equal vigor to regain the individual and corporate freedoms that have been surrendered to government and to highly organized groups.

In short, we must help to revitalize the private areas of our economy.

For companies, this means maintaining a business climate that encourages free enterprise. For individuals, it means regaining the degree of freedom that nourishes individual initiative.

This is a formidable task, but it can be done if businessmen wake up to their political responsibilities.

Perhaps this can be done through existing channels. Perhaps it will require the setting up of our own task forces to come up with a positive program for free enterprise—for conserving the basic values of our society. There have been excellent results whenever this approach has been used. Among the most outstanding examples are the Hoover Commissions, the Business Advisory Council, and the Executive Reserve of the Business and Defense Services Agency. But however we move, we must move decisively.

In the process of stepping up our political activity, however, we must never overlook the growing importance of our state and local governments. Everyone in management must work to convince local and state officials of the desirability of a favorable business climate. If communities look upon a company merely as a good tax base they can cripple its ability to compete or force it to move to a more favorable part of the country.

Here, too, the accent will be on people. Big Democracy means Big Government, and Big Government breeds Big Bureaucracy. Bureaucracy, in turn, generates inefficiency. If we want *efficient* Big Government we are going to need Big Men—and industry must furnish its share. We can no longer afford to lock up our corporate brains in a political isolation booth.

LABOR-MANAGEMENT RELATIONS

We have talked at some length about managers as a group and about employees below the management level as a group. But what about their relations with each other? Our chances for a prosperous decade would be vastly improved if labor and management could achieve a higher degree of cooperation.

We have made considerable progress in this direction.

No progressive businessman today denies the basic merits of unionization nor the many positive features of the union movement. Unions have a vital role to play in our society and that role should not be underestimated.

But unions have an equally important *responsibility* to their members and the general public. Like other institutions in our rapidly changing society, unions are in a curious period of transition. Trends in population, technology, and worker skills will inevitably force our unions to change their goals, their methods, and their philosophy. They, along with management, must adapt to a new era of competitive standards and changing markets. For both labor and management, flexibility and adaptability will be keys to survival in the Sixties.

The situation today is far different from what it was twenty-five years ago. During the Thirties unions were fighting for their lives. They needed militant leaders and aggressive programs. But long after the need for them had passed, these militant characteristics of the union movement were retained—for that matter, they are with us today. As a result, wages have risen much faster than productivity; supplemental benefits have become an abnormal part of employment costs; and management's right to manage has been hemmed in by restrictive work practices. The pattern of bargaining has been one of demanding more and more at each negotiation regardless of the economic consequences.

Added to these demands have been jurisdictional disputes and an intense competition among union leaders to prove who could get the most for his membership.

The time has come when union leaders must show a greater sense of statesmanship and assume a role of greater public responsibility. What American industry needs today is an increased ability to compete. *Make no mistake: If we cannot compete, no amount of union pressure can bring back employment, increase security, or generate the job opportunities needed in the future.* And to compete we need better labor-management cooperation.

The big question is, how can we bring about a constructive change in labor-management relations? Obviously, there are no pat answers, but here are some sensible courses of action.

First, we must communicate with our employees to make sure they understand that the Sixties will be a very competitive period—one that will require flexibility in the duties of each individual and wholehearted dedication to the company's survival and profitability.

Second, our employees must be encouraged to take a more active interest in union affairs. Union meetings must no longer be run by small cliques who stay in power because of the inactivity of a majority of the members. Given the facts, the average employee is a bulwark of common sense. If he becomes a vital force in his union, we can expect—and achieve—greater understanding and realism.

Finally, we must find a way of reconciling the union movement with the public interest. Unions represent the greatest private power on earth. They can shut down entire industries and dictate who can work, under what conditions, and at what wage. They can press for wages that exceed known productivity levels and insist on work practices that seriously limit operational flexibility. They can push for fixed-cost benefits without relating them to the economics of the industry. And, they are free to engage in direct political activity that extends their power far beyond their immediate membership.

Something must be done to give them public responsibility commensurate with their power. As I see it, this can be done in two ways: through constructive legislation or through better internal leadership.

It would be far better if union responsibility came about internally by means of responsible leadership. This would keep another area free from government intervention and within the competitive framework of our American system. But let me stress again that constructive legislation will be required if responsible union leadership fails to materialize.

I hope that this will not be necessary. Free collective bargaining, based upon the realities of the economic situation, is one of the best guarantees of a prosperous decade.

SUMMARY

We have covered so many different problems and suggested solutions that I would like to sum up the salient points for your further consideration.

First, we must become customer-oriented. We must work as never before to make the consuming public an ardent fan for our products or services.

Second, in industries such as ours, we must make sure that we will have an adequate supply of reasonably priced raw materials when we need them. This means that more money and manpower will have to be poured into exploration and development, and that more money and ingenuity will have to be channeled into developing low-grade sources of these materials.

Third, we must expand our research activities. But we must be sure that they pay their way—producing with reasonable frequency the new products and materials which will loosen the customers' purse strings and create new markets.

Fourth, we must overcome the cost-price squeeze by becoming completely modern in all phases of our operations. This means using the most efficient tools, the least wasteful practices, and the most up-to-date production methods.

We are in the early stages of a new industrial era that promises to be even more revolutionary than the old: the era of *automation* and *electronic equipment*. If we master these new tools, American industry will maintain its lead among the nations of the world. I say if—but we have no alternative. We must put automation and computers to work for us.

Some people worry about the effect of automation on jobs—the old fear that machines put men out of work. But our industrial history proves that machines ultimately create many more jobs than they displace and that the problems they raise are transitory in nature.

It is more realistic to worry about what would happen if we *did not keep pace* with technical progress. If Europe automates faster than we do—or, worse still, if Russia does, I leave to your own judgment the effect on our position in world markets.

Customer orientation, adequate raw materials, intensified research, and improved technology are essential ingredients for a prosperous decade; but, important as they are, we will fail unless we achieve a more constructive use of our human *resources* and a greater awareness of human problems.

Much of the responsibility falls on management. If we do our job well, the decade ahead in all likelihood will be a prosperous one. If we do not, it will be our own fault because the opportunities are there right along with the problems.

This is a tremendous challenge. If we meet it successfully we will have improved ourselves, our companies, and our country, and will have helped to make democracy and free enterprise ever more clearly the road to survival.